OVERCOMER

OVERCOMER
Cinderella Fosberry

*An Iraqi woman's true story
of faith, and courage*

XULON PRESS

Xulon Press
2301 Lucien Way #415
Maitland, FL 32751
407.339.4217
www.xulonpress.com

Unless otherwise indicated, Scripture quotations taken from the King James Version (KJV) – *public domain*.

Printed in the United States of America.

ISBN-13: 978-1-54563-536-0

I dedicate this book to my Lord and Savior and give Him all the glory. It is good to speak of the signs and wonders the most high God has wrought toward me. How great are His signs and how mighty His wonders. His kingdom is an everlasting kingdom, and His dominion is from generation to generation.

To every brokenhearted person and suffering soul, to the one whose cross seems too heavy to bear, and to the one of whom the world is not worthy, I pray that every word in this book will be a word of hope, healing, redemption, and direction. I pray that you will draw closer to His heart, His love, and His peace.

A REAL-LIFE STORY

C inderella Fosberry is a Christian woman who lived in Iraq through the dark times of war and loss. Despite the suffering she faced, she chose to follow the Lord Jesus Christ, walking by faith and overcoming all obstacles.

In this book, she shares many testimonies of following the Lord not only in Iraq, but also in other countries of the Middle East:

- She shared the gospel and prayed with Uday, the oldest son of Saddam Hussein, the former president of Iraq.
- She left her family and country in obedience to the Lord's call to minister in Sudan.
- She risked her life to share the gospel with the president of Sudan, Omar al-Bashir.

- She was questioned and thrown into prison in Jordan because of her faith in Jesus Christ.
- She stood before King Abdullah of Jordan and shared the message of hope, peace, and salvation.
- She witnessed many miracles.

In this book, Cinderella Fosberry shares with her readers biblical stories and devotionals that the Lord gave her for encouragement, strength, and comfort in her darkest hours and through many long, sleepless nights.

Like Cinderella, all Christians will face trials and tribulations, but God has called us to overcome by the blood of the Lamb and the word of our testimony.

Table of Contents

Chapter 1

Beauty for Ashes

To give unto them beauty for ashes.

Isaiah 61:3 (KJV)

M y story begins in Iraq, a country where God Almighty has been glorified throughout history. We read in the Old Testament book of Genesis that the Garden of Eden was located in Iraq. We also read that God called Ibrahim (Abraham) to leave his family and land in Ur, the modern-day Iraqi city of Nasiriya, and follow Him by faith.

In the book of Jonah, we discover the story of Nineveh, or Mosul in today's Iraq. We read the word of the Lord came to Jonah, but because of his resistance, the Lord sent a great wind on the sea to direct him to his destiny. The Lord provided a huge fish to swallow Jonah, but he was released

1

when he prayed a powerful prayer from inside the fish: "I cried by reason of mine affliction unto the Lord, and he heard me; out of the belly of hell cried I, and thou heardest my voice" (Jonah 2:1-2, KJV). The story concludes with the repentance of the people of Nineveh, a wonderful story of God's mighty power and love.

In the book of Daniel, we discover the prophet Daniel lived in Babylon in present-day Iraq. In that country, he received most of his prophecies. In a land that did not know the true God, Daniel fearlessly stood for his faith in God and refused to bow to other gods. He kept his faith even when it cost him life-threatening persecution and resulted in being thrown into the lions' den. There, the deliverer, the Lord of heaven's army, showed up to save him by sending His angels to close the lions' mouths.

In the book of Daniel, we also read about Shadrach, Meshach, and Abednego. Friends of Daniel, they too lived in Iraq, and when they refused to bow to the king and worship him, they were thrown into a fiery furnace. Praise the Lord, however, because the Babylonians saw a fourth man walking in the fire with them, who was the angel of the Lord, the Son of God, the mighty one. Not only was our Lord glorified by saving them, but as we read in the book of Daniel, not even was the smell of smoke on the young men when they came out of the fire. The only thing the fire did was to burn the ropes so they could come out free. Hallelujah! Praise our mighty God and Savior!

You or your loved one might be in the fire right now, but trust that the Lord will deliver, protect, and keep you. He will save.

Shadrach, Meshach, and Abednego asked the Lord to bless them in their captivity in Babylon, and the Lord answered their prayers by taking them higher through the fire. Through the fire, they reached their destinies. Through the fire, they were set free from bondage. Through the fire, they were purified. I love the song "Through the Fire" by The Crabb Family, which says:

He never promised that the cross would not get heavy and the hill would not be hard to climb.

> He never offered a victory without fighting, but He said help will always come on time.

Just remember when you're standing in the valley of decision and the advisory says give in.

Just hold on, our Lord will show up, and He will take you through the fire again.

I once heard a story of a man who refined gold for a living. He started by selecting a dark piece of gold and putting it into a glass. Then he lit a fire under the glass to melt the metal. Gradually, he turned the fire higher, causing the metal to melt even more and the impurities to be removed. Only the man knew when it became 100 percent pure gold; no one else knew the season or the time required. Once he saw that the gold was ready, he turned off the fire and removed the gold. Smiling, he looked down and pondered the beautiful work he had just created.

"It's ready and pure—100 percent gold," he announced.

If you could have asked him, "How did you know it was ready?" he would have answered, "Because when I looked at it, it was like a mirror. I could see my face in it."

This is how the Lord molds us. Sometimes He puts us into the fire, and sometimes He sets the flame higher until he can see His face in our lives. When we become like a mirror reflecting the light, the love, and the glory of our creator, then He turns off the fire because we are pure and ready to serve Him.

This is a principle that the prophet Job experienced. After all his losses, he proclaimed, "But he knoweth the way that I take: when he hath tried me, I shall come forth as gold" (Job 23:10, KJV).

The fire we walk through is meant to break our bondages by burning up the things that are blocking the blessing of the Lord in our lives. The fire will burn up lust, love of money, and the desire for material things or worldly positions. It will destroy whatever is holding us back, so that we can say, "I am crucified with Christ; nevertheless I live, yet not I, but Christ liveth in me" (Galatians 2:20).

The fire, trials, hurt, and pain that we experience are meant to purify our hearts and change us to become like Jesus—to love others like Jesus did, to forgive like Jesus forgave, to bless others like Jesus blessed. Then our lives will bring a message of healing, hope, and love to everyone around us. The fire is a bridge taking us from where we are in life to where He wants us to be. It leads us to our destinies, leading us from ashes to His kingdom, as we read in Isaiah 60:1–2: "Arise, shine; for the light is come, and the glory of the Lord is risen upon thee, for, behold, the darkness shall cover the earth, and gross darkness the people; but the Lord shall a raise upon thee, and his glory shall be seen upon thee." God wants us to rise from the ashes of our pain, our hurt, and our circumstances to the beauty, light, and glory He will shine upon us.

I first learned the idea of beauty for ashes from my name. When I was born and my mother first laid eyes on me, tears of joy flowed and she said, "I am going to call her Cinderella. May her dreams come true, and may she live happily ever after." I love my name for what it has taught me. The first part of my name is *cinder*, which means "burnt, ashes, or dust." The second part of my name is *ella,* which means "a bright light." The pain, tears, fiery trials, and ashes I endured led me to discover my destiny, which is to reflect the light and love of Jesus Christ to everyone around me. I am called to be *ella*, even if there are cinders in my life. I am called to be Cinderella.

I'll end this chapter by sharing something I love. Hundreds of years ago, when God's people were captive in Babylon, the captors asked God's people for a song. As we read in Psalm 137:

By the rivers of Babylon, there we sat down, yea, we wept when we remembered Zion, we hanged our harps upon the willows in the midst thereof, for there they that carried us away captive, required of us a song, captors asked of us a song; and they that wasted us required of us mirth, saying, "Sing us one of the songs of Zion."

The captors in Iraq, in Babylon, asked God's people for a song; their hearts (the captors) were thirsty and hungry for the songs of the Lord. They needed a song of hope, a song of comfort, a song of peace. Today, hundreds of years later, my people, the Iraqi people, still need to hear the songs of our Lord, we need the Lord's glory—His peace, love, and salvation—to shine again upon our country.

Yes, Iraq has been through war, loss, and death. Yes, it was destroyed by its enemies. However, I grew up knowing that it's a country that God's glory will shine upon again. The Lord will give Iraq beauty for ashes. It has been blessed in the past and always will be. God bless Iraq.

Chapter 2

Count It All Loss

And I count all things but loss for
the excellency of the knowledge of
Christ Jesus my Lord; for whom I
have suffered the loss of all things,
and do count them but dung, that I
may win Christ.

Philippians 3:8

L iving in Iraq as a Christian posed many challenges. I grew up constantly seeing death around me. I witnessed many painful things such as explosions, bombings, and women dressed in black because they were mourning their loved ones lost in war. We all lived in fear, knowing each day could be our last.

In the middle of all this distraction and pain, I heard many voices. Many of them were explosions, fear and negativity, but one voice changed my life forever. It was my mother's voice—a voice of hope and faith expressed through her prayers.

My mother was a true believer and follower of Jesus Christ. When the first war began in Iraq in 1980, she was terrified but found refuge in our Lord and Savior Jesus Christ. In Him she found the hope and peace she longed for. She began reading the Bible, attending church, and trusting in God's promises.

When I was a little girl, every time I was afraid due to war, she comforted me by saying, "Cindy, God has told us in the Bible, 366 times, 'Do not be afraid.' He gives us this promise for each day of the year, so every day that we wake up, no matter what we are facing, the Lord tell us, 'Do not be afraid.'"

She filled my heart with many truths from the Bible:

"Fear not; for thou shalt not be ashamed. Neither be thou confounded; for thou shalt not be put to shame, for thou shalt forget the shame of thy youth, and shalt not remember the reproach of your widowhood anymore."

Isaiah 54:4

"For I the Lord thy God will hold thy right hand, saying unto thee, 'Fear not; I will help thee.'"

Isaiah 41:13

"Be strong and of good courage. Fear not, nor be afraid of them. For the Lord thy God, he it is that doth go with thee, he will not fail thee, nor forsake thee."

Deuteronomy 31:6

Fear not; for I have redeemed thee, I have called thee by thy name; thou art mine. When thou passest through the waters, I will be with thee. And through the rivers, they shall not overflow thee. When thou walkest through the fire, thou shalt not be burned; nether shall the flames kindle upon thee, for I am the Lord thy God. The holy one of Israel, the savior, since thou wast precious in my sight, thou hast been honorable, and I have loved thee.

Isaiah 43:1-4

God is our refuge and strength, a very present help in trouble. Therefore we will not fear, though the earth be removed, and though the mountains be carried into the midst of the sea, though the waters thereof roar and be

troubled, thou the mountains shake
with the swelling thereof. The Lord
almighty is with us; the God of Jacob
is our fortress.

Psalm 46:1-3

Oh, hallelujah, what a Savior! He will never
leave us nor forsake us. He was our refuge
and strength in the days of war, in the days of
trouble in Iraq.

I remember in 1991, when I was about thirteen
years old, we were not allowed to leave our homes
because of the planes that bombed us. Many people
thus fled Baghdad and went to underground refugee
shelters. At that time, it was too dangerous to leave
home even to buy medicine or food.

Nonetheless, my mother would tell me, "Cindy,
we are not going to wait for everything to be safe
and normal before we go to church. We are going
to church today to learn about the Lord and to worship and pray."

I remember her holding me by my hand as we walked two hours to the church and another two when we returned home. We were so hungry and thirsty to learn more about the Lord, to worship Him, and to fellowship with other believers that we went to church even when there was bombing, blood, and dead bodies all around us.

Today many people say that they cannot go to church because they are too busy, the weather is too bad, or they are going shopping or taking a vacation. There are so many excuses people come up with for skipping out on church. However, we should never take the blessing of going to church or serving the Lord for granted, especially in a country where the Lord has provided freedom, churches, Bibles, pastors, and Christian books to help us in our spiritual growth. We did not have these blessings in Iraq.

We were willing to risk our lives to go to church, and worship and serve the Lord. With every step we took, we risked our lives. My mom often told me that the Lord was like an umbrella, giving us shelter. Danger would pass by us, she said, but it would not touch us. "For in the time of trouble he shall hide me in his pavilion; in the secret of his tabernacle shall he hide me; he shall set me upon a rock" (Psalm 25:5).

My mother's prayers for me and my siblings were not for our safety or for us to obtain a good education, worldly position, or even a happy life. All her prayers were for us to be in God's will, led by His mighty hand to serve Him by serving others and sharing the love, hope, and healing of Jesus Christ.

As a little girl, I knew only one thing: that we were all created for a reason, a purpose. However, most of us are plagued with asking *why*: Why war? Why death? Why famine? Why pain and suffering? We ask the Lord for answers and for solutions, and the Lord replies, "You are my answer to humanity." He created you and me for a purpose. In the midst of the darkness of this world, even while we are walking in the valley of the shadow of death, the Lord will anoint us and fill us with His light, love, and power to spread His message of grace, hope, healing, and salvation.

I surrendered my life to the Lord at an early age. All I wanted was to serve Him, but I faced many challenges. First, Iraq is an Islamic country, with ninety-nine percent of the population Muslim, so it was against the law to share the gospel or give out Bibles. Serving the Lord publicly was dangerous; it could cost believers their lives. My pastor was thrown into jail just for having a prayer meeting in his home.

Second, being a woman in my country posed many challenges too, since women lacked freedom of choice in many decisions affecting their lives.

Third, I was young, in my last year of high school, when I went into ministry full-time, and I did not have enough education to do all I wanted to do. However, all these challenges faded away when the Lord spoke to me through 1 Corinthians

1:27: "But God hath chosen the foolish things of the world to confound the wise, and God hath chosen the weak things of the world to confound the things which are mighty."

This Scripture touched my heart deeply. I knew then that I didn't need to be strong or educated, possess money, or live in safety in order for the Lord to use me. He does not call the qualified; instead, He qualifies those whom He calls. For example, when He called David to serve Him, everyone was surprised at the choice. They thought the Lord would choose one of David's brothers because they were strong, educated, and mighty. The Lord, however, chose David because he had a heart filled with love, humility, and songs of worship.

The Lord cares about our hearts—how much we love Him and others. As 2 Chronicles 16:9 says, "The eyes of the Lord run to and fro throughout the whole earth, to shew himself strong in the behalf of them whose heart is perfect toward him."

The Lord calls us to serve Him, and He will show us His strength, might, and glory. He gave us the power of the Holy Spirit, as Acts 1:8 says: "But ye shall receive power, after that the Holy Ghost is come upon you: and ye shall be witnesses unto me both in Jerusalem, and in all Judaea, and in Samaria, and unto the uttermost part of the earth." With this power, we are promised we can do amazing things. This is the same power given to Peter and John, mere fishermen who had no education and were not qualified. Although they were poor fishermen, with the power of the Holy Spirit, they turned the world upside down.

As a young believer, I didn't know where to start, so I started on my knees every day, asking the Lord to direct my steps. I began serving the Lord in a home related to Mother Teresa's ministry. We would love, feed, and shelter orphans and disabled children who had been rejected by their families. We also spread the message of hope and salvation in hospitals and jails.

Everywhere the Lord directed me, I followed. When we serve the Lord, not only are we changing other people's lives, but we too are changing and soon realize that the only thing worth living for is what we give to others.

I always believed that with God all things were possible, but the people around me constantly discouraged me, saying, "Oh don't do that; it's dangerous," or, "You're young," or, "You're a woman," or, "No one will give you permission for that." Nevertheless, I believed God's promises, not people's opinions, and the Lord was faithful to honor every step I took.

One day I got a phone call from one of the most famous schools in Iraq (Dijlah), an all-girls school with approximately a thousand students. They said, "Cinderella, we have heard you are a Christian and love the Lord. Could you please be a teacher in our school to teach the girls about the Bible and Christianity?"

This was a dream come true; I couldn't believe it. Even after I told them I hadn't gone to college yet, they still wanted me, and I began teaching seven classes a day. That was a miracle; the Lord opened a door that felt impossible to open.

After that, one day I saw a big theater on TV called Zayona Theater. As I looked at the thousands of people seated in this theater, I prayed I could minister in that place one day. In my heart, I wanted God to be glorified there. I wanted to invite people from all churches, denominations, and religions to gather in one place to worship our Lord, pray, and hear a message of hope.

However, I questioned myself: "How can I do that? Where do I start? Where will I get the money to rent the place? They will never give me permission to rent the theater because it is against the law to share my faith publicly." The Lord used the story of Joshua to encourage me and to answer all my concerns. It was a lesson learned and a principle I still use today in my Christian life.

As leader of Israel, Joshua did not experience the same miracle that Moses did. Moses saw the Red Sea open and viewed the road in front of him. He then started walking on the miracle that the Lord gave him. It was different for Joshua, however. When the Lord instructed him to lead the people across the Jordan River, there was no miracle yet. I am sure Joshua thought if he put his feet into that water and started walking, he and his people would drown. Nevertheless, the Lord told them to start walking, and Joshua and God's people obeyed the Lord and trusted His voice. Then the Lord gave them their miracle; with every step they took, the waters divided, and there was a road they could walk on.

The Lord's word to me was, "You may be afraid of waters that could drown you, but when you start walking in faith, I will start opening the way for you and make a miracle for you."

This is the same principle that He gave in Mark 16:17–18: "These signs shall follow them that believe; in my name shall they cast out devils, they shall speak with new tongues, they shall take up serpents, and if they drink any deadly thing, it shall not hurt them; they shall lay hands on the sick and they shall recover." When we start walking in faith and obeying the Lord, signs and wonders will follow us.

After that, with every step I took, the Lord opened doors. First, this public theater gave me permission to rent the place. Second, all the people we invited accepted our invitation—Catholics, evangelicals, and Muslims. Thousands of people attended these revival meetings. Third, the Lord provided all expenses for renting the place, buying Bibles to give the people, and for buying gifts for the kids who attended the meetings. To be able to do the first two meetings, my mom and I sold our jewelry and we used the money for the meetings. After that, the Lord provided for us in many miraculous ways. He never left us nor forsook us; He was our provider and blessed us richly.

Do you think the Lord needs our money or our stuff? He is God Almighty and owns heaven and earth. The Lord wants our hearts; He wants us to give Him all that we are.

Sometimes while serving the Lord, we will face loss, rejection, or temptation. Sometimes we will feel tired, confused, and alone. When that happens to you, I encourage you to kneel at His cross and sing with me this song:

> Everything I once held, dear Lord, I count it all as loss.
> Lead me to the cross where your love poured down.
> Lead me to my knees, Lord, I lay me down.
> Rid me of myself; I belong to you.

I encourage you to lay down every dear thing and count it all as loss. You and I belong to Him— not to a family, a person, or a job. We don't belong to money or success or even our children. We belong to Him and thus surrender our lives, plans, futures, families, and time completely to Him.

Chapter 3

Praying with the Oldest Son of Saddam Hussein

Give the king thy judgments, O God, and thy righteousness unto the king's son.

Psalm 72:1

When I was eighteen years old and living in Iraq, the most dangerous person in our country was Uday Hussein, the oldest son of Saddam Hussein. Everyone feared him because of his cruel acts, and everyone recognized how evil he was. Uday committed even more crimes than his father, so everyone labeled him an evil monster.

One night he sent hundreds of his army, armed with swords, to kill women who were involved in prostitution. They cut off the heads of hundreds of women, and when everyone woke up the next morning, they saw the heads in the bloody streets. No one could explain why he would do such an act; he did it just because he appeared to enjoy killing people.

If Uday entered a shopping center, a restaurant, or even a home, he had the right to shoot whomever he wanted and to rape any woman he wanted. He tortured, raped, and killed many people. In the United States, he was on the news many times because of his cruel acts and violent behavior. Hollywood even made a movie about him, showing how evil he was and telling the story of his violent acts.

One day in 1997, Uday was the object of an assassination attempt. He was shot in his leg but survived. However, he was sick and hurt for a while, lying in a hospital bed and fighting death. At the same time, all the people were happy—even Christians—because they believed he had finally gotten what he deserved. The people believed he would die and his evil acts against the Iraqi people would end.

During this time, the Lord told me, "Cindy, I want you to love him and pray for him."

That was the easy part of the story. It was easy to be compassionate toward him and pray for his salvation from a distance. However, one day while praying for him, the Lord said to me, "It is not enough to pray for people. It is not enough to love people. I want you to go and share my love, my Word, and the message of salvation with him."

I replied to the Lord, "Lord, how can I do that? I will be killed. Lord, this man and his family made the laws in this country, which say that we cannot publish Bibles or give them away. How can you want me to go to him, the son of Saddam Hussein? He will kill me, and he will kill my family."

I continued, "Lord, how about you send the pastor? He's a man of God; he can die for you—not me."

The Lord answered, "No, Cindy, I want you to go."

I gave the Lord many excuses, reminding Him that I was young, afraid, and a woman. How could I possibly reach him? However, deep in my heart, I knew I had to obey the Lord, so I tried to encourage myself.

I asked my brothers and sisters in Christ to pray for me, but they merely laughed and said, "You are just a crazy teenager. God would never ask you to do a crazy thing like this. This is not from the Lord, and you are just putting yourself, your family, and your church in great danger. We will not pray for you or support you, because you are going to get everyone killed."

Discouraged, I returned home and got on my knees, crying and praying to the Lord. I felt lonely, with no one believing in me.

Then I heard the Lord say to me, "The dangerous thing to your Christian life is if you don't go and stay home instead. It might look safe, but that is the real danger: to not obey me and to not be in my will. The safest thing for the Christian life, and in your life too, Cindy, is to be in my will and in my hands. You may be in dangerous places among dangerous people, but you are always safe in my arms."

In that moment, I wiped my tears away and thought, *What is the worst that could happen to me?* True, they could torture me and cut me into pieces. They could put me into jail, burn my family's home, and kill me and my family. But praise the Lord, nothing in this world could separate me from the love of Jesus Christ. I had something that no one could take from me, and that was the love of our Lord. As Romans 8:35–37 says:

> Who shall separate us from the love of Christ? Shall tribulation, or distress, or persecution, or famine, or nakedness, or peril, or sword? As it is written, "For thy sake we are killed

all the day long; we are accounted as
sheep for the slaughter." Nay, in all
these things we are more than con-
querors through him that loved us.

I answered the Lord: "Lord, I will obey you.
Even if that's the last thing I ever do for you, I will
obey you."

The next day I went to the hospital where Uday
lay. I had no appointment and no contacts to put me
in touch with him prior to our meeting, so I went to
the hospital by faith, relying on the Lord's promise
in Isaiah 45:1–2. That passage of Scripture says:

Thus saith the Lord to his anointed,
to Cyrus, "Whose right hand I have
holden, to subdue nations before
him; and I will lose the loins of
kings, to open before him the two
leaved gates; and the gates shall not
be shut; I will go before thee and

make the crooked places straight;
I will break in pieces the gates of
brass, and cut in sunder the bars
of iron."

Arriving at the hospital, I immediately encoun-
tered police officers at the front gate, holding
machine guns in their hands. I couldn't go any far-
ther into the hospital without getting past them, so
I confidently said, "Hi, I need to meet Mr. Uday."

They looked at me, laughed, and said, "You,
you, young lady?" to which I answered, "Yes, me."

They informed me that people from the government, Saddam Hussein's family, and other relatives
had come to see him, but not been allowed into his
room. "So who are you that you think we will let
you in?" they asked.

I responded, "Okay, I'll tell you the truth. The
Lord sent me to deliver a message to him; I have a
message from the Lord to Mr. Uday."

This confused them because they had never heard such a thing. They answered, "Do you mean the Lord our God, or do you mean the Lord of a church?"

I said, "Yes, I mean the Lord our God, and if you call Mr. Uday and tell him that, I know he will let me in."

They said, "Okay, we will. Just give us a minute."

They grabbed their phones and called the hospital. In just a few minutes, they turned around, looked at me, and said, "This is a real miracle. It's really God, because he agreed to meet with you. He's sending his personal car to get you, and he wants to hear what you have to say."

The car quickly arrived. It was the most elegant car I had ever seen and featured beautiful curtains. It was so cool. I rode in the car with my big bag filled with Bibles, so happy that the Lord had opened the doors before me so I could do what He had called me to do. Soon the car pulled up to the hospital.

Anyone who would have looked at me in that moment might have said, "Wow, what a strong young Christian girl—going to die for her faith in Jesus. How courageous, what faith."

But the truth is, as the car approached the hospital, I was so terrified that my legs shook uncontrollably. I started thinking about what might happen to me if Uday didn't like what I shared.

In that moment of fear, the Lord whispered to me, "Cindy, why are you shaking and scared to meet the son of Saddam Hussein? Why are you shaking and scared to meet the son of a president? You are the daughter of the King of kings and Lord of lords."

When I heard His voice, all fear and doubt faded away, and all the thoughts with which Satan was trying to fill my mind disappeared. I felt God's mighty power wash over me, and I enjoyed a new confidence, knowing I was the daughter of the most Highest, the daughter of the King of kings and Lord of lords. This position was even higher than the position of Uday himself.

"I want you to know that you are a child of the almighty King, no matter where you are in life or where He might send you. Wherever you go, serve, and minister, even when facing your greatest fear or darkest night, you are equipped with heavenly strength, power, and peace from your Father, the King of kings and Lord of lords."

When I arrived at the hospital, I met people whom I had seen on TV, people who worked for Saddam Hussein and were known as terrorists and killers. I was surprised when they approached me, saying, "We heard you have a message from the Lord. Can you tell us about it? We need to hear this kind of thing; we need to hear about the Lord."

When I entered the hospital, I recognized it was the worst place ever and a dangerous place to be. Nonetheless, I knew the people here needed the Lord's love, forgiveness, and peace. As we read in the book of Romans, where sin abounds, grace does much more abound.

The spirit of the Lord moved upon this dark place. Everyone wanted to know about the Lord, so I shared my faith, prayed with them, and gave away Bibles. The people's eyes filled with tears, so hungry and thirsty were they for true love, for the truth. They didn't need someone to judge them; they needed God's grace and truth to set them free, and that is what I believe happened that very day.

I entered Uday's room and saw him lying on his bed. I greeted him and gave him a Bible as a gift. He greeted me in return, then looked up toward heaven and said, "Lord, talk to me."

He then opened the Bible, and it fell open to Psalm 119. I believe this Scripture was exactly what he needed to hear. He read maybe six to seven verses, and as he was reading, I kept saying, "Amen, amen" in agreement with the Word.

When he was done, he closed the Bible, kissed it in a show of respect, and said, "What is your message?"

I shared the gospel with him, the love of our Lord toward him. I told him it didn't matter what he had done or where he was in life. It didn't matter what people thought of him or what he had done to other people. The Lord would meet him wherever he was and touch his life and give him a new heart. He could be made new, for the Lord makes beautiful things out of the dust.

Before judging anyone—even Uday Hussein— read through the Bible and see those God chose to save, heal, bless, and forgive. You might be surprised.

In Genesis 29:31, for example, we read that God chose Leah. When the Lord saw she was hated, He opened her womb. The Lord knew she was hated, weak, and unloved, but when He saw her rejected and crying at the lowest point in her life, He opened her womb. Even if you are at the lowest point in your life, He will reach out to you and give you your greatest miracle.

I love how He chose Rahab, a prostitute. When she proclaimed her faith in God, the Lord saved her life. When Joshua and Caleb entered the city of Jericho, the Lord told them that everything in that city would perish, but Rahab and her family would be saved. What happened to all the religious people in the city? They perished. What happened to the women of good deeds? They also perished. What about all the wives and good mothers? Like the others, they perished. But God saved Rahab the prostitute because she called on His name.

When all my friends were saying, "Don't go to Uday. He doesn't deserve risking your life for; he's a sinner who has hurt many people," my answer was the word that the Lord spoke about Saul in the New Testament. In that story, the Lord called Ananias to go pray with Saul, even though Saul had been responsible for much evil committed against the saints. The Lord encouraged Ananias to go anyway, saying, "Don't be afraid, because he's chosen and ready and prepared to hear the message of love, forgiveness, and salvation."

Too often we judge people by their actions, by their behavior, by what our eyes can see. However, our Lord sees deeper than that. He knows our hearts with all the details of our stories—all the pain, the suffering, and the circumstances that only He, our creator, can know.

The Lord has chosen you for His glory and His purpose. You might be drowning in the waters of sin, pain, and rejection, and every religious person is telling you to swim harder or giving you directions to get out. Maybe the people closest to you are questioning how you let yourself fall into these waters in the first place. But praise the Lord, Jesus, when He sees you drowning, will immediately jump into the deepest waters and hold you in His loving arms. He will look at you with eyes of love and say, "Are you okay?" He doesn't care where you are; He cares about how you are.

Jesus will reach out to you at your lowest and weakest point and rescue you. Show Him your greatest weakness, and He will show you His mighty power. Show Him your greatest need, and He will show you His abundant provision. Show Him your greatest sickness, and He will show you His wondrous healing.

After sharing with Uday about the Lord, I asked if he wanted me to pray with him. He answered, "Yes, please pray for me."

When I finished praying, he said, "You know what? I was hurting from my sin, from what had happened to me in this accident. Many Muslim leaders and religious people from all denominations came to visit me. They tried to comfort my soul, bringing all kinds of gifts to lift my spirits."

He paused for a moment to point to these gifts scattered all around the room. Some of the gifts featured Islamic verses. The Catholics had given him a statue of Mary, and he had received many other gifts as well.

He continued speaking: "None of these things comforted my heart, but the words you shared from the Bible did. I know now the source of true healing. It's Jesus Christ."

Rejoicing in the Lord, I exclaimed, "Amen! Hallelujah!"

Despite my joy, I didn't know what was coming next. In my mind, I was still questioning this situation and my position. I wondered, "Am I going to jail? Is this real? What's going on?"

This man was known for raping girls, kidnapping, and killing people; however, even though I was only a few feet away from him, he never looked at me in a threatening manner. I felt there were angels standing between him and me the entire time I was with him. In faith, I could see the angels providing a wall of protection. In fact, this is exactly what the Lord has promised us in Psalm 91:11: "He shall give his angels charge over you, to keep you in all your ways." The glory of God covered that place.

Before I left, Uday said to me, "Cinderella, whatever you want, you can ask me for it and I'll give it to you—home, cars, money. I own Iraq, and I will give you anything that you or your family needs."

I responded, "You don't need to pay anything for your salvation or for Jesus' love. Jesus' love is free, and I came today to share it with you. It is free, and you don't need to pay anything."

He then requested his personal car to take me home; he also gave me his personal phone number and asked me to call him if I needed anything.

After that meeting, two times on record, he provided food and medicine for a full month to support Christians around Iraq. Two times on public TV, in a country where ninety-nine percent of Muslims don't believe Jesus was crucified, he talked about Jesus and the cross. Hallelujah!

Many people ask me today, "Do you really think that Uday was saved that day? Was his prayer sincere?"

I don't know the answer to that question; only God does.

As Christians, we are called to proclaim the Word of God—a word of redemption, healing, and deliverance. One day that word will either save them or be used against them in judgment. In 2004, the day before Uday was killed in Baghdad, I prayed that the Holy Spirit would remind him of the words he heard on that day when I visited him. One day, I believe, we will all be surprised at the ones we see in heaven.

I want to encourage you today that God may call you to share the gospel with someone who is hard to reach out to. You may feel it impossible that they would accept your message. However, when you think that something is too hard or impossible, when you consider a situation to be hopeless, you are actually bringing God Almighty down to your image, thoughts, and limits. God created all of us in His image, and He is mighty in power. He can do all things; nothing is impossible for Him. Remain in

God's image—thinking as He thinks, loving as He loves, forgiving as He forgives. Believe that you can do all things through Christ who strengthens you.

Let's overcome our fear and always remember that we are the children of the most high God. Let's go with this power and strength to our families, neighbors, and cities and proclaim the message of love, hope, and salvation.

Chapter 4

Meeting with the President of Sudan

While serving the Lord in Iraq during the rule of Saddam Hussein, one day as I prayed, the Lord showed me a vision of African children and adults. I did not know who they were or where they were from, but I began to pray for these faces that the Lord showed me. After a few days, the Lord told me, "I want you to leave your family and country and go to Sudan."

Needless to say, I was quite surprised. I thought, *How can I do this? It's impossible*. At that time, it was shameful in our culture for an unmarried woman to leave her home and country. Some close-minded families might even kill their daughters for such an act. Understandably, I feared telling my dad, who was already abusive and against my faith.

47

This call was hard to obey; it felt impossible because Sudan was a country where Christians were being persecuted. Furthermore, it was a different culture with people of a different color. I had no money to get there and no connections to make it happen, but I knew deep in my heart that the Lord who called me would make it happen. He would be with me, and I would rely on His promise in Hebrews 13:59: "He hath said, I will never leave thee nor forsake thee." If He was with me, then He would be the source of everything I needed during this journey.

I prayed to have Abraham's faith. I'm sure when the Lord called him to leave his country and family, he had questions. More than likely, he was afraid, having no clue as to where he was heading. He faced his family, culture, and the danger of the wilderness, yet he overcame his fears and doubts and followed the Lord by faith. Like Abraham, I overcame my fears and negative thoughts, knowing if I obeyed the call, the Lord would bless my journey.

I read Genesis 12:1–2, which states: "Now the Lord had said unto Abram, 'Get thee out of thy country, and from thy kindred, and from thy father's house, unto a land that I will shew thee: And I will make of thee a great nation, and I will bless thee, and make thy name great; and thou shalt be a blessing.'"

Immediately, I surrendered to His will and said, "Lord, I will go to Sudan. I will go wherever you send me. I will carry my cross and follow you to the rest of my life."

Then I prayed and fasted for three days. On the third day, I approached my father and said, "Dad, I have to ask you for something," to which he answered, "Sure."

I continued, saying, "God has called me to go to Sudan."

He laughed at me and said, "Sure, you can go."

Astonished, I replied, "Really?"

He responded with a challenging look in his eyes. "Yes, you can go, but under one condition:

that your God provides for this trip. If He is real and provides, then I'm okay with it because it will mean God really has called you to go."

I accepted the challenge and began praying for my need, which was huge. It would take a lot of money to cross the border, buy food, and provide for the other traveling needs and expenses of the ministry. However, in three days, a miracle happened. Christians and other people I knew suddenly started calling me and saying, "The Lord told me to give you a hundred dollars, or "The Lord told me to sell my jewelry and give you the money." By the third day, I had all the money I needed to leave Iraq and get to Jordan.

Before my dad came home from work, I laid all the money on the couch where he could see it, and when he entered the room and saw the money, he asked, "What is that?"

I said, "You said if my God was real, He would provide. He is real, and He provided. He will take care of me, so can you please let me go?"

To my delight, he responded, "Yes, you can."

However, one problem remained. I could not leave the country without being accompanied by a male relative; it was against the law. While praying about the situation, one night I dreamed of my uncle, whose name was Jeffery. I saw him walking and heard the Lord say, "This is Samier."

Not knowing the meaning of the name, I looked it up when I awoke and discovered it is an Arabic name that means "the man who walks with you in a night journey."

A little later in the day, my uncle's wife called my mom and said, "Jeffery just got an order from work. They gave him a mission to leave Iraq and go to Jordan."

This meant that my uncle, who was a pilot, was traveling to Jordan and could take me with him. Praise the Lord, he agreed to my plan, so I left Iraq and began making my way to Jordan. Because of the war, we had to go to Jordan first. A no-fly zone was in effect, so no airplane could leave Iraq. My uncle and I, therefore, had to drive to Jordan, and from there I would fly to Sudan.

After I arrived in Amman, the capital city of Jordan, I quickly realized the entire journey would be by faith. I was staying with a family from church, but after a few days, they said, "We cannot let you stay in our home any longer. We have some needs, and it's too hard on us for you to stay."

I left with my suitcase in hand and went to a place called the Second Circle. There was a church nearby, and I sat down and began to cry. It was getting dark, I had nothing in my pocket, and I was hungry, homesick, and scared. I prayed, "Lord, you told me you were going to be with me like you were with Abraham. Lord, I need you. I'm alone."

It was then I remembered what the Bible says about my Savior in Matthew 8:20: "And Jesus saith unto him, 'The foxes have holes, and the birds of the air have nests; but the Son of man hath not where to lay his head.'"

If the King of Glory did not have a place to lay His head, then I knew He could help me get through this. As the Bible says in Hebrews 2:18, "For in that he himself had suffered being tempted, he is able to succor them that are tempted."

While meditating on these thoughts, a woman touched my shoulder and said, "Are you Cinderella?"

I acknowledged I was, and she stated, "I have been looking for you in church." She looked me in the face and asked, "Why are you crying?"

I replied, "I don't have a place to stay, and I'm scared. I have to stay in Jordan because the Lord has called me to go to Sudan."

She told me, "This is why I was looking for you. The Lord told me to find you and take you to my home and treat you like my daughter until you go to Sudan."

That is exactly what she did.

My next challenge was to find a connection in Sudan. The Lord opened the doors one after another until finally, after some hard times in Jordan, my traveling expenses were provided, and I was connected to a family in Sudan. After many delays, I finally reached my destination. God's promise to me came to pass, and I rejoiced greatly as I stood in a church in Sudan between my brothers and sisters in Christ. It was a dream come true.

At that time, Sudan was a country known for killing Christians. Some of the Muslims there were armed with weapons and specifically targeted Christians.

I lived through some of the cruel acts the army committed against Christians. Several times they came into the church and the orphan center and pinned us against the wall while they pointed guns at us and questioned the pastor.

I heard many stories of pain and suffering, of churches being burned and preachers and missionaries killed. I witnessed the "torture tents" made for women who were caught attending church. The idea was to pull these women and their children out of church, take the women to the tent, tie them up, and whip them forty times. No matter the conditions around them, these brave women chose to come to church, to worship and serve, knowing that they could be killed. All these acts were commands from the President of Sudan, Omar al-Bashir.

After a few months of I had begun serving the Lord in Sudan, the Lord told me, "Cinderella, I am going to give you a mission before you leave this country."

I told the Lord I would do anything He wanted me to do.

The Lord's voice then said to me, "I want you to go and share the gospel with the president of Sudan, Omar al-Bashir."

I protested, "Oh Lord, how can I do that? He's known for killing Christians; he will kill me for sure."

Then I remembered the Lord had been with me in Iraq and in Jordan, in hard times and in troubled waters. He had faithfully been with me, protected me, and delivered me from all danger. I knew He would do it again.

I started praying for the president and tried to meet with him. I went many places and filled out numerous applications, but the doors remained closed. For three months, there was no progress.

Then one day when I was at church, someone walked up to me and said, "Cinderella, I found the president's sister's address. We could try to visit her; maybe she could make the connection."

Since I had started praying for the president, many times I had considered returning to Jordan, especially when all doors seemed to close. I began to lose hope, but many times in my dreams I saw the president saying, "Cindy, I need Jesus. Cindy, I need help." I felt in my spirit that he was suffering and needed to be encouraged with a word of hope and peace.

My friend and I proceeded to the president's sister's house. We knocked on the door, and she allowed us to come in. I asked to meet with her brother, and she nicely called the president's home on my behalf. However, she was told there was no way we could have meeting with him.

Though I was disappointed, I knew there was a reason I was with the president's sister. We had a great conversation about faith; I also prayed with her, gave her a Bible, and then left. The next day, however, I had a strong feeling to return to her home, so I did. When I arrived, two guards at the gates saw me and said, "Oh, thank God you came back. The president's sister left a letter for you and asked us to give it to you if you showed up again."

The letter stated, "Dear Cinderella, I will not be home for a while, but I want you to know that I have arranged a meeting for you with my brother, the president of Sudan. This is the date and directions to the president's home, and all the details."

Overjoyed, I began to jump up and down in the middle of the street, exclaiming, "Hallelujah, praise the Lord!" I was so happy and rejoiced that nothing was impossible for my God.

On the date given, I arrived for the appointment and entered the president's home. I waited a while for him to appear, and when he entered the room, I was so scared. He was a large man, his facial expression angry, and I knew he killed Christians. I was terrified, saying in my heart, "Lord, this is a big mountain I can't face." I don't know why, but I kept comparing him with a big mountain.

The Lord immediately reminded me of the verse in Zechariah 4:7: "Who art thou, O great mountain? Before Zerubbabel thou shalt become a plain."

Maybe I saw him as a big mountain, but before our God's name, he would become a plain.

He drew closer to me, his face still angry, and said, "What do you need? You have only a few minutes, so say what you want."

"Can you give me more time? Can we sit and talk?"

"No, I have other appointments. I thought you just wanted a picture and that's it."

"No," I said, "I came today to talk to you about Jesus."

It was only by the name of Jesus—the name that was given all power in heaven and Earth, the name that my favorite song extols:

> At your name
> The mountains shake and crumble
> At your name
> The oceans roar and tumble
> Angels will bow down
> The earth will rejoice
> Your people cry out
> Lord of all the earth
> We shout your name, shout your name . . .
> Yahweh, Yahweh, we love to shout your name, O Lord.

that this angry man who killed Christians grabbed me by my hand and said, "Come on, daughter. Let's sit down. I need to hear about Jesus."

Before I could say anything, he said, "I have many problems in my life, many battles I am facing. Can Jesus help me? Can He do something for me? Can He save me?"

I answered by reading a chapter from the book of Psalms that talks about God's blessing to the king, and how he can be blessed if he chooses to believe and walk by faith. The president's eyes filled with tears, and we talked about how everything in his life—his presidency, family, money, and everything else he had—could be lost in a blink of an eye, but when we surrender our lives to our mighty God and His purposes, we gain that which is eternal. We prayed together, and he asked if he could have the Bible I was reading from. Of course, I agreed, and he took the Bible and hid it under his robe so that his guards and family would not see it.

He said, "Please keep praying for me, because I am tired."

I shared more about Jesus, who said, "Come to me, all you who labor and are heavy laden, and I will give you rest."

I returned home, and we all celebrated and praised the Lord.

After that meeting, the president issued a new statement announcing a new law that is still practiced in Sudan today. The new law said all Christians were free to practice their faith. They could go into the streets to distribute Bibles, and they could openly share their faith. They were allowed to build churches, and no one could hurt them.

We were so excited at this news that we immediately went into the streets of Sudan with a big truck filled with Bibles. As we rejoiced in our freedom, we saw a police car coming toward us. At first, we thought it was a trap, that they were coming to arrest us or kill us; instead, they said, "Don't be afraid. Every time in the past, the president sent us to stop you and arrest you, but this time he sent us to protect you while you walk and share your faith in the streets. Your gospel message is a message of love and peace and forgiveness, and we need that in our country."

I believe that by the power of the name of Jesus, we can overcome every mountain. No matter how big it is, no matter that it feels as if it will never crumble, our God is greater, stronger, and higher than any other god. If our God is with us, who can ever stop us? If our God is for us, what can stand against us?

Chapter 5

Biblical Overcomers

In this chapter, I will share a few stories from the Bible that helped me to overcome, encouraged me in my Christian walk, and gave me hope in my darkest nights. From these stories, I learned several important principles about being an overcomer in the Lord.

1. To be an overcomer, we must be in covenant with the Lord.

One of the most powerful stories in the Bible that picture a life with a covenant is found in the Old Testament. There we read of a covenant between King David and Saul's son Jonathan. Years after this covenant of friendship was established, Jonathan died. The story states that King David asked his servants, "Is there anyone left from Jonathan's family that I can bless?" He wanted to bless Jonathan's seed because he remembered the covenant he had made with him.

The servants answered King David: "Yes, there is a son, but he is lame."

They wondered what the king would do with a lame boy. He would not be of any use in David's kingdom since he obviously could not fight in battle.

However, King David said, "I have a covenant, and that's all that matters," so they brought the lame boy to the king.

King David looked him in the eye and said, "Son, fear not, because I am going to do you a favor. Because of the covenant I made with your father, I am going to return to you all of your father's lands that were stolen by the enemy. Plus, you will eat bread at my table, the king's table, forever."

Today the Lord will look into your eyes and say, "My child, I have a covenant with you by the blood my Son shed on the cross for you. By this covenant, by this amazing grace, I will return all that the enemy has stolen from you. I will fight for you, and you will be seated at the table of the King of kings. I will feed you every day and forever with blessings."

You may be thinking, "Oh Lord, I am crippled, weak, rejected, addicted, angry, hurt, and unloved. I am unworthy of this unconditional love." Yes, the Lord knows where we are in life. He knows our hurts and struggles, our failures and limitations, but because of His covenant of love, He will seat us at His table and feed us with His manna so that we can grow strong and overcome. He will return what the enemy has stolen. He will restore our lives.

2. To be an overcomer, we need to live by faith.

In Hebrews 11:23, the Bible says, "By faith Moses, when he was born, was hid three months of his parents, because they saw he was a proper child; and they were not afraid of the king's commandment."

Moses' mother, with faith in God, hid him and did not fear. By faith she saw what other people could not see: God's mighty hand around her baby. By faith she trusted that those hands were powerful enough to work the impossible in her life. As a result of her faith, while all the other male children were thrown to their deaths in the river, her little Moses was saved and kept alive.

Do you think having that kind of faith was easy? Just imagine the first three months of this baby's life. Like any other infant, he cried and fussed, was gassy, and had many sleepless nights. I think it likely his mother did not sleep at all, since she had to keep the baby quiet so that the Egyptians would not know that he was alive. With every tear she shed, she held on to her faith and hope that God would do something to save her and her child. Every time she heard the other mothers crying for their children, I am sure she thought, "I'm next," but by faith she kept her eyes upon the Lord and not her fears.

The Bible promises if we keep our eyes on the Lord, we will never be put to shame. God honored the faith of Moses' mother in two ways. First, she has been remembered throughout history as a woman of faith, a woman who overcame the most difficult situation imaginable by her faith in God. Second, her faith was instilled in her child's life, as we see in Hebrews 11. After mentioning his mother's faith in one verse, this chapter mentions Moses' faith not once, not twice, but many times. Whereas Moses' mother overcame by faith in one situation, her son lived the lifestyle of an overcomer. Facing life's challenges in faith will not only affect our lives, but it will also affect the people around us,

Hebrews 11:24–28 says, "By faith, Moses, when he was come to years, refused to be called the son of Pharaoh's daughter, choosing rather to suffer affliction with the people of God than to enjoy the pleasures of sin for a season. By faith he forsook Egypt, not fearing the wrath of the king."

By faith, by faith, by faith—and if we could ask him, "Moses, where did all this faith come from? How did you overcome all the challenges you went through?" he would answer, "My mother."

3. **To be an overcomer, we need to surrender our lives to the Lord.**

Exodus 2:3 says, "When she could no longer hide him, she took for him an arc of bulrushes, and daubed it with slime and with pitch, and put the child there, and she laid it in the flags by the river's brink."

This verse touched my heart and helped me to overcome in many situations. Moses' mother did all she could to save her child's life. She prayed, she had faith, and she did many other things, but she came to a point when she realized she no longer had control and had to lay this situation at the Lord's feet.

Our God often begins His greatest miracle in our lives when we come to a similar point. We think, we plan, and we try to solve our problems with worldly wisdom. We think perhaps we should ask someone to help us, or maybe we need to try harder. However, the Lord wants us to realize we have no control of the situation. The moment that Moses' mother laid him in the basket was the moment when the Lord carried the situation. When she laid him in that basket, she was not sending him to a day care, to his grandparents, or to a nanny.

She understood fully that this could be the last time she would see her son's beautiful face, but she knew she had no other choice but to let him go.

In that agonizing moment of surrender, she was an overcomer. By laying her situation at the Lord's feet and giving Him all control, she was giving the Lord space to work wonders. In response, the Lord did for her what she could never do for herself. In similar fashion, if we want to overcome overwhelming obstacles in our lives, we must lay everything at His feet, surrendering all control and trusting His wisdom, mighty power, and amazing love.

At the end of the story, we see Moses' mother once again holding her baby in her arms. Miraculously, a conversation between Miriam (Moses' sister) and Pharaoh's daughter resulted in his mother being called upon to serve as a wet nurse for him: "Shall I go and call to thee a nurse of the Hebrew women, that she may nurse the child for thee?" (Exodus 2:7).

Oh Lord, how amazed I am about every detail in your Word!

God is never late to deliver us from our pain; He is always on time. As a mother, I know if you don't nurse your baby for a day, the milk starts drying up. But hallelujah, Moses' mother's milk was still fresh and warm, and she was able to nurse him. Trust Him in your darkest season; He will always be on time—His perfect time.

After Miriam spoke to Pharaoh's daughter, she ran home to tell her mother the good news.

"Mom, Mom, Mom!" she likely called out.

Hearing her daughter's urgent voice, Moses' mother probably thought, "the baby is dead," or "the baby has drowned."

I want to encourage you that when you are hopeless, expecting the worst news, always remember the Lord wants to take your life and fill it with more blessings than you can imagine.

Miriam's news to her mother was good news, however. "Mom, the baby is alive!" she exclaimed.

We see the scene quickly shift for Moses' mother. First, she was broken and afraid, but now she was overcome with joy at God's working for her good. How great is our God! When she was at her lowest point, He was with her, comforting her, even while He prepared the miracle to complete her story of overcoming.

Here stood a woman, at the lowest point in her life, called before the highest authority in the nation. Pharaoh's daughter said to her, "Take this child and nurse him for me, and I will give thee thy wages."

Not only was her son back with her, but also, she was going to be paid for taking care of him and nursing him.

Similarly, God will not only return whatever you surrender to Him, but He will also bless you with wages, extra blessings, and miracles. Everything you've been praying for, surrender to Him. Give all control to Him and He will not fail you. He will help you to overcome.

4. To be an overcomer, we need to know God is with us no matter the circumstances.

One of the most powerful stories in the Bible helped me to overcome during a painful season in my life. It's the story of Hagar, a maid with no rights. She had no life of her own and no voice to protest her harsh treatment. Eventually she came to a point when she said, "I can't take this anymore. I am tired, worn-out, a slave to my masters. I will flee."

She then ran away into the wilderness, with nothing but a broken heart. While she was there, the voice of the Lord called her, saying, "Hagar, Sarai's maid . . ."

Not only did He know her name, but He also knew her painful situation. He understood her burden, her problem. It was though He was saying, "I know you are a maid. I know you have no rights or privileges. I know you are suffering and humiliated."

Interestingly, God then instructed her to return to her mistress and submit under her hands. In essence, He said, "You go back; I know it's hard, but you'll overcome. I'll give you a son, a blessing, and you will call his name Ishmael to remind you that I heard your cries and saw your afflictions."

Many times, I have tried to run from situations that the Lord has allowed into my life. Sometimes my trials don't make sense and I don't understand why, but I have learned that I have to trust Him. Sometimes we need to stay under the pain and hurt for a season, but even in that hard season, He is with us and will give us a blessing.

Always remember, He knows your name, your pain, and your story. He will give you a blessing (Ishmael). The Lord has seen your afflictions and heard your cries. An overcomer is not a person who has a perfect life, but someone who overcomes all obstacles by trusting God and His purpose for their life.

After the wilderness encounter, Hagar learned no matter the circumstances, she could overcome with God at her side.

Years later, she was again lost in the wilderness, but this time Ishmael was with her. Running out of water, she knew she and her son faced certain death. She lifted up her voice and wept because of the hopeless situation. Then God opened her eyes and she saw a well.

She exclaimed, "My God sees me. He's a living God who sees me wherever I am."

Let's be like Hagar and trust the Lord to empower us to overcome in any situation. Let's pray this prayer from our hearts: *Open the eyes of my heart, Lord, so I can see you, the living water. All I need is you and your presence. It is not by power or might, but by your Spirit that I can overcome and do all things through Christ who strengthen me. Amen.*

5. To be an overcomer is to be rooted in Christ.

As a little girl, I was familiar with the story of Samson; however, I thought it was a story of defeat. In my mind, it was a story of a powerful man who started his journey well but ended up weak and broken. When I read the story now, as an adult, I see a story of overcoming, restoration, and redemption,

Samson's hair represented his power, and after it was cut, he became physically weak.

Then he was blinded by his enemies, humiliated and broken at their hands. Gradually, over time, his hair began to grow out again. Interestingly, the enemy could cut his hair, but they couldn't destroy the roots. In similar fashion, we might lose our vision and glory, but if we are rooted in Christ, we will overcome all losses.

The story of Samson is not a story of tragedy, but rather a story of hope and overcoming. There is always hope, no matter the situation. If your "hair" has been cut, just remember, it will start growing again. Your purpose and vision will be restored. Hallelujah!

Chapter 6

My Prison Testimony

Then said Jesus unto the disciples,
"If any man will come after me, let
him deny himself, and take up his
cross, and follow me."

Matthew 16:24

After serving the Lord in Sudan, I returned to Jordan and began ministering. Some other people and I started an underground church by offering to teach English for free. Many people wanted to learn English, and the book we used was the Bible. I believe in the power of the Word of God. It changes us, helps us, directs us, and gives us hope. After studying the Bible with them, we witnessed many wonders. People were set free, renewing their minds and lives.

Soon after this revival in the ministry, one day when I was at home, a man from the police station arrived and asked if I could go to their office to answer a few questions. I was nine months pregnant at that time, sick, and on medication. I thought, *Let me go and see what they want,* not expecting anything bad.

I went to the station, praying the whole way there, and as soon as I entered the office, the officer began writing something on paper and questioning me. I still did not know what was going on until they began spitting on me and cursing. They said they knew some other people and I had started an underground church and were bringing Muslims to the Lord Jesus Christ; that was against the law in their country.

Despite their threatening tone, I felt powerful, as if I were standing on a rock. As I always say, I was not standing *like* a rock, but I was standing on *the* Rock. We will never be shaken as long as we stand on the Rock, Jesus Christ. Everything else may be sinking sand: our jobs, families, even the most precious things in our lives. The only stable thing we can stand on is the Lord Jesus Christ. As a well-known song says: "On Jesus Christ, the rock I stand, All other ground is sinking sand."

First Corinthians 10:4 also speaks of this rock: "For they drank of the spiritual rock that followed them, and the rock was Christ." Hallelujah, Christ is our rock!

The interrogators said they were going to kill my husband, and tears began falling from my eyes. The police then led me to a prison cell, spitting on me, pulling and pushing me toward the space. They threatened to take my baby as soon as he was born and warned I would never see him again. That terrified me, and with every step I took toward the prison cell, I grew more fearful.

"My family, my ministry, my dreams, my Christian family—why, Lord, are you taking away everything in my life?" I cried out silently.

"My, my, my"—I was thinking only of myself.

When the door of the cell opened, I saw hundreds of women sitting on the floor, and in that moment, I heard the voice of the Lord saying, "Welcome to the ministry of Jesus Christ. Do you really want to serve me? Do you really want to minister to people? Then carry your cross and serve me. This is a dark place, and I want you to let them know about the light of Jesus Christ."

An overcomer doesn't think about himself or his own needs, but about what truly matters in this life: people who are dying every day without hearing the Word of God, people without hope. When I entered the room, all the women quickly surrounded me; each one of them began to tell me about the crime she had committed. Some said they were there for drugs, and others were there for prostitution. There were many other reasons given as well, and soon they asked me, "What is your crime?" I shared with them my crime: loving and serving the Lord. That was how I gained the opportunity to share the gospel with them. Everyone was singing, praising the Lord, and praying. I would not describe it as a jail at that time; it was more like a church. It was a revival.

During this time, a miracle happened. Someone called the police station and said, "Let Cinderella out." Supposedly, this person was a congressman in the government. Now, in that part of the world, if you know someone from the government, your oppressors will let you go free; they will do whatever he asks them to do.

After I was finally free, I witnessed to everyone: "I don't know how this happened. I don't know anyone in the government, but my friend is the King of kings and Lord of lords. Hallelujah, He delivered me from jail and He always delivers me from all troubles. I trust Him."

During the next year, they kept bringing me in and out of jail. They confiscated my passport, as well as my husband's, making each day a challenge of faith. We knew we could go to jail or be killed at any moment. The United Nations heard about our story and helped us come as refugees to the United States. The Lord took something that could have killed us and through it gave life and hope for our family and our ministry. The devil tried to bring evil against us, but God turned it around for good.

Whenever you are faced with trials or tribulations that are meant to harm you, always remember that God is going to turn them around for His glory and your good. "But as for you, ye thought evil against me; but God meant it unto good, to bring to pass, as it is this day, to save much people alive" (Genesis 50:20).

Chapter 7

The Healing Story of My Son

And with his stripes we are healed.

Isaiah 53:5

After I left the jail, I celebrated my freedom. I was still in Jordan at that time, and David, my first boy, was one year old, just learning to crawl and walk. It was early in the morning, and my husband was out in the ministry while I was at home. In our country, we use big stoves that are unstable and move easily when touched. I was boiling a pot of water in preparation for a dinner with believers who were coming to our home that day. It was a typical blessed day, cooking for my friends and family.

I did not notice David had crawled into the kitchen. He opened the oven door, putting his weight on it, which caused the stove to fall over and the pot of boiling water and its contents to fall on him. My baby was stuck under the stove, his head caught between the floor and the stove.

Hearing his screams, I ran into the kitchen and quickly realized the boiling water had poured upon him. Also, because the gas under the stove was exposed, the gas tank opened and my baby was burned. My soft and tender one-year-old son was trapped in a horrible, life-threatening situation.

I tried desperately to pull David out, shoving the stove and gas tank back into place. My baby suffered broken bones in his head, and all of the skin on the right side of his body was burned and melted away. His eyes, ears, and shoulder were bleeding. I thought to myself, *He is dead! That's it!*

I had no phone and no car, so I ran outside, screaming for help. A neighbor responded and drove us to the first hospital we saw. Crying uncontrollably, I raced into the hospital, and what I asked them surprised even me.

I didn't ask, "Will you treat my son?" but instead I pleaded, "Please give my son pain medication and numb him so he will die without pain."

I felt sure he was dying, so the only thing I could think of was to ask for pain relief. It was so painful and so miserable that anyone who saw him would have wept.

The medical personnel merely looked at me and responded coldly, "Don't you know the rule in this country? You have to pay five hundred dinars (which is equal to seven hundred American dollars) just to get into the hospital. You have to pay this amount first before you can be seen or treated."

I begged them, "Please, I will give you my passport—anything—just treat my boy. I will give you the money later; just give me time."

At that time, not only did we not have the finances for this, but we lived by faith daily. We usually had only a few dollars at a time, sometimes not even having milk to feed our baby. We lived in faith step by step.

"We will get the money; the believers will stand with us," I explained.

The man I was speaking to said, "We are sorry. Just go cry outside the hospital."

Brokenhearted, I walked back to the front door of the hospital, holding my baby close to me, and called someone from the church. From early that morning till late that evening, I waited at the door of the hospital for someone to come to my aid. My son, half of his face burned, fainted frequently, and each time I thought he was dead. Then, to my great relief, he would wake back up and start to cry.

I didn't know what to do. I was alone, without the seven hundred dollars I needed and without anyone to comfort me. I prayed to the Lord, "Lord, you have a reason and purpose for allowing this to happen. If you want to take David home to be with you, I want you glorified in it. If you want him to live with half a face and with wounds, I want you to be glorified. And if you heal him, as I know you are able, I want you to be glorified."

A deep and comforting peace from heaven filled my heart. This was the same peace experienced by the woman in 2 Kings 4:26. In that verse, we read Elisha instructed his servant, "Run now, I pray thee, to meet her, and say unto her, 'Is it well with thee? Is it well with thy husband? Is it well with thy child?' And she answered, 'It is well.'"

In the Hebrew language, "it is well," or "peace," is translated from the word *shalom*. As I stood there with my suffering son in my arms, I had that same peace (*shalom*).

While I prayed, the Lord was at work. The Christians tried to collect enough money for the hospital. Later that night, they came to the hospital and paid the money; my son was admitted, and we stayed for two weeks. Thank the Lord for the church, who gave generously to help meet our needs.

That was the greatest time of my life. All the doctors, nurses, and people in the hospital who had never had the chance to hear about Jesus now received the opportunity. The glory of God filled the hospital. Sick people asked us to pray for their healing in Jesus' name. Others participated in Bible study with us. We would often sit with these people until 4:00 a.m.

God not only answered my prayers and was glorified in the ministry we did in the hospital, but He also healed my son. David is seventeen years old today. God touched his eyes, ears, face, and body and healed him completely.

The doctors said, when we left the hospital, "He will have these scars forever."

But I prayed and said, "Lord, I know you are able to heal his face."

I didn't want him to go through life with all these scars. The doctor warned us that when a person's scalp is burned, hair will not grow there again, but all of David's hair grew back.

You may be as I was—with no money and no one who understands, weeping in the pain of your circumstances. Maybe you are alone with no one to comfort you. However, I want you to know that even when there is no one around, Jesus is there. I know He is standing beside you because I visited His grave and it is empty. Hallelujah, He is alive! He is always with you to wipe away your tears, to hold you, to comfort you, to make a way when there seems to be no way. He will take care of you.

While I was at the hospital, I sang a song all day long that goes like this: "When the world says it's over, the Master says, 'No, I have just begun.'"

When the world tells you it's over, when your husband tells you it's over, when your doctors tell you it's over, when your bank account tells you it's over, or when your wife or children tell you it's over, the Master and Savior, the King of kings and Lord of lords, says, "No, I have just begun."

He begins great and mighty things when we feel all alone. In the lowest point of our lives, He looks at us and says, "Now you are ready for the new level—for healing, abundance, and blessings."

When David was eight years old, kids would sometimes say mean things because of a few scars remaining on his back, hand, and shoulder. It used to pain me, but I prayed the Lord would use this in a positive way. One day, I saw David standing in front of the mirror. He took his shirt off, opened his arms wide, and stared at his scars. He had tears in his eyes, but also a big smile on his face. I recognized the same joy and peace that I had experienced when standing by the hospital door.

I asked my son, "David, why are you crying and smiling at the same time?"

"Mom, I am so happy and so proud that I have these scars on my body."

"David, why are you so proud of them?"

"Because every time I look at them, I remember that Jesus touched me and healed me."

Today you might be healed, but still bear some scars. These scars don't hurt or bleed anymore, but they are there. I want you to learn a message from this little boy named David. Even if you have some scars remaining from your past, look at them and say, "Thank you, God, for these scars, because every time I look at them, I remember you healed me, saved me, and delivered me."

Chapter 8

Standing Before the King of Jordan

For such a time as this.

Esther 4:14

When I was in Jordan ministering, the Lord spoke to my heart and commanded me to pray for the king of Jordan, King Hussein. While praying for him, I heard the news that he had died. I cried and said, "Lord, you told me I was going to meet him and share with him the message of salvation. You promised me."

The Lord then reminded me that He is faithful in keeping His promises and said, "Pray for his son, the new king, King Abdullah II."

So, I began praying for him and believed for a quick answer from the Lord to meet him. However, what ended up happening was that I prayed day after day, month after month, and year after year without seeing an answer. People whom I had asked to pray for me questioned me, saying, "Was that message really from the Lord?" They asked this question because it seemed to be taking a long time for the Lord to answer.

Many times, the Lord gives us promises, but they do not happen as quickly as we thought they would. Don't ever doubt that God gave you His promise. It is God, but sometimes it takes time. We have to believe God's timing is best and that He will fulfill His promises in our lives. Many times, in my personal life, I have had to trust in Him and believe in His timing.

With everything, there is a time and a season. We may not know the time, but God knows. We just have to trust Him and keep praying and waiting. Isaiah 40:31 says, "But they that wait upon the Lord shall renew their strength; they shall mount up with wings as eagles; they shall run, and not be weary; and they shall walk, and not faint." So, I kept praying for the king of Jordan, King Abdullah II. Even after coming to the United States, I kept praying. For eight years, the Spirit in me could not stop praying for him.

I then returned to Jordan for a women's conference and took two American pastors' wives with me. One morning I took a taxi downtown to purchase some items.

The taxi driver casually remarked to me, "You won't believe what I saw."

Curious, I asked, "What did you see?"

"The king of Jordan. He is in Abdoun Circle, an area here in the capital. I just saw him there."

"Were there people around him?"

"Yes, his guards were all around him, and some people were waving from afar."

"Please turn around and go there. I want to see him," I quickly said.

He then drove me to Abdoun Circle, but to our surprise, there was no one there. However, what caught my attention was the presence of security vehicles, Hummers. These vehicles were used to protect the king, so I knew he was still around somewhere. I started praying, asking the Lord to lead me in the right direction.

It had just begun to rain, and there were a lot of restaurants in the area. I said, "Lord, you have to lead me. Which restaurant is the king in?"

The Lord guided me to a certain Chinese restaurant, and when I opened the door, I immediately saw the king of Jordan sitting at the farthest table. He was eating dinner with his wife, Queen Rania. All the tables around him were filled with security personnel.

As I looked at the guards, my mind was flooded with the memories from when I was in prison. I knew these people could take me to jail, hurt me, or hurt my family. I was scared, but I knew I had to walk in faith—not by what I felt, but by what the Lord had told me.

I walked up to the security detail and said, "Hi, I just need to talk with the king."

As expected, the security man said, "No, get out. You cannot bother the king. That is why we are sitting here: to keep people away. No one is allowed near him."

I asked again and he refused again, so I turned to find a place to pray. Sitting at a table, I prayed, "Lord, you have to lead me. What is your plan? What are we going to do? It is now or never. This is my chance. He is just a few feet away from me; I have to do it."

The Lord instructed me to pick up the menu. It was a large paper, with one side containing the menu, but the other side blank. The Lord told me to start writing, so I began writing a message from the Lord to the king; when I finished, I folded it up and held it in my hand.

The Lord then instructed me, "Whenever the king stands up to leave, even if the security detail is surrounding him, just push them away and go forward and begin speaking."

I started praying, and I waited for the king to leave.

As soon as the king stood up, all of the guards surrounded him. Holding their machine guns, they formed two lines around him. In some Middle Eastern countries, if anyone tries to get too close to a president or king, the guards will shoot immediately, fearing that the person has a bomb or is trying to attack. They don't care; they will just shoot.

As the king began walking out of the restaurant, I found myself beside him. The guards obstructed my path, but the Lord told me to push through them. I knew it was not by my strength, that there were angels surrounding me and helping me, because the security personnel moved so easily when I pushed against them to get to the king.

I stood in front of the king and boldly said, "Your Majesty, I have to talk to you."

Looking at his guards, he made a sign with his hand and said, "Let her speak."

I began telling him a story that I had heard from many people about his dad's mother. This quickly drew his attention. The woman was sick, but before she died, an American missionary told her about Jesus. She prayed and was saved.

I concluded the story, saying, "Do you know why your kingdom is blessed beyond the other countries in the Middle East? Because your grandmother prayed the prayer of salvation for Jesus to come into her life. I am sure that she prayed for you to know the Lord Jesus as your personal Lord and Savior, and for Him to bless your life. I believe that you are blessed because your grandmother prayed for you in the name of Jesus."

The king and his wife responded as if they were interested, drawing closer to hear what else I had to say. I shared the gospel with them and took a picture with them.

When I finished, the king said, "I appreciate your prayers and for coming to tell me this message." He took the letter that I had written for him and said, "I promise I am going to read this letter."

After I left the restaurant, I could not stop praising and worshiping the Lord. Yes, I was happy about the letter, the meeting, the conversation. All these things were great, and it was an amazing day. The only thing I could do was fall on my knees, lift my hands, and worship our great God. I could not stop thinking of His love, power, greatness, and faithfulness.

If you have any situation that you have been praying for, and it feels as if there is no answer, just know that in God's divine timing, it will come to pass. He will be faithful in answering your prayers. Even when it takes a long time, if you keep believing and praying, He can take impossible things and make them possible. He sent the taxi driver my way, He led me to the restaurant, and He showed me favor, allowing me to stand before the king. As Isaiah 60:22 says, "A little one shall become a thousand, and a small one a strong nation; I the Lord will hasten it in this time."

I believe the Lord has called us for such a time as this. Esther 4:13–14 reads:

> Then Mordecai commanded to answer Esther, "Think not with thyself that thou shalt escape in the king's house, more than all the Jews. For if thou altogether holdest thy peace at this time, then shall their enlargement and deliverance arise to the Jews from another place; but thou and thy father's house shall be destroyed: and who knoweth whether thou art come to the kingdom, for such a time as this?"

The Lord will give us heavenly courage to reach the people around us with the message of grace and salvation. He has promised He will give us favor before them, like He did for Esther. I pray for all women to have the spirit of Esther, the spirit of courage and faith.

Chapter 9

Jonathon: My Little Miracle

*I shall not die, but live, and declare
the works of the Lord.*

Psalm 118:17

In the midst of the revival that took place in my life and ministry, the enemy suddenly attacked from every side. He came in as a flood of trials in my life. However, Isaiah 59:19 encourages us that "when the enemy shall come in like a flood, the Spirit of the Lord shall lift up a standard against him."

The enemy attacked so strongly that my life was shaken. The devil always tries to shake our lives and distract us, but what he doesn't know is that every attack and distraction helps us learn how to fly higher in our faith. The little eagle in its nest is fed, protected, and comfortable. As soon as that nest is shaken, however, the little eagle is forced out of its nest—its comfort zone—and must fly. In the process of learning how to fly, it falls many times; but the parent eagle quickly flies under the little eagle and lifts it up until it learns. I would venture to say there has never been a baby eagle that died from falling, because he was always lifted up by his parents.

I praise the Lord that we have a strong eagle—our Lord—who, when we start falling because of the attacks of the enemy, flies faster than our fall. Each time, He lifts us up on His wings and takes us higher until we learn how to fly. As Exodus 19:4 says, "Ye have seen what I did unto the Egyptians, and how I bare you on eagles' wings, and brought you unto myself."

As my life was shaken, I fell into deep despair. I was depressed, I was hurt, and I was at one of the lowest points in my life. But praise the Lord, I experienced what Leah in the Old Testament experienced. The Bible says, "When the Lord saw Leah, that she was hated, he opened her womb" (Genesis 29). He did something special for her—not when she was strong or holy or reading her Bible regularly, not when she was strong in her faith, but when the Lord saw her rejected and hurt. When He saw her in her pain, He opened her womb and gave her a miracle, something she could rejoice in even in the midst of her darkest time.

At that time in my life, I already had two boys, and medically, I had only a one percent chance of getting pregnant again. One night while I was lying in bed praying, tears falling from my eyes, the Lord gave me the verse about Leah.

It was as if the Lord told me, "I see you hurt, rejected, and attacked, but I am going to give you a blessing. I have opened your womb to give you joy in this time."

I believed what the Lord spoke to me, so the next day, by faith I went to the doctor and said, "I need to have a pregnancy test."

Not long after, he said, "Congratulations! You are pregnant."

"Amen, what a miracle!" I responded, rejoicing with the blessing that the Lord had given me.

On my second appointment, however, the doctor said, "The baby is positioned in the wrong place, and its growth is not progressing."

The doctors called my condition a right cornual pregnancy (ectopic pregnancy) and said I needed to abort the baby for my own health and safety. I was sick and bleeding, and they gave me an emergency pass to the hospital, warning me that I could die at any time because of the severe bleeding.

I believed the Lord had given life to this baby. I decided—even if the baby was in the wrong place, even if it meant I would die—I would obey God and not abort this baby. I chose to die obeying God than to live knowing I had disobeyed the Lord just to take care of myself and my health. I chose to trust the Lord that He would take care of me and the baby, believing the entire situation was under His control.

On another one of my doctor visits, they did an ultrasound and said the baby was dead. He wasn't growing, and they couldn't find a heartbeat. I then went to five other doctors, but they all agreed that my baby was dead. Heartbroken, I believed it was over and I now had to abort him.

I was sitting in the doctor's clinic, my mother beside me. When the nurse went to get the medicine to prepare me to abort my dead child, the voice of the Lord came clearly to me: "Cindy, leave this place right now. Don't believe the doctor's report. I gave this baby life. Keep proclaiming life over this death situation."

I quickly left the clinic, but everyone said I was being emotional, I was crazy, what I was doing made no sense, and now I would die and leave my other two children motherless. This was not wise, they cautioned. But I closed my ears to all the voices around me and kept listening to the voice of my Savior and healer, Jesus Christ. John 10:27 says, "My sheep hear my voice, and I know them, and they follow me." I knew my Savior, and I recognized His voice. In faith, I continued speaking His Word and His promises, rejoicing in them.

Finally, as my health deteriorated, I told my husband, "Take me back to the United States. That is where the Lord is leading me."

We returned to the States, and I went to another doctor. When they performed an ultrasound, the baby's heartbeat was loud and clear. Tears began falling from my eyes, and I said, "But I was told this baby didn't have a heartbeat and was in the wrong place."

They assured me, "No, this baby is alive. He has a heartbeat, and he is in the right place. Everything is great."

As Christians, we need to keep our eyes upon the Lord, listen to His voice, and believe in His plans. We must not be distracted by the enemy, people's opinions, negative reports, or worldly wisdom.

If we keep our focus on the Lord, our lives will be lightened and we will never be ashamed. As Psalm 34:5 says, "They looked unto him, and were lightened: and their faces were not ashamed."

Keep looking higher to the Lord Almighty, looking to His heavenly plans for your life. Believe them, and soon they will come to pass. I pray that everything that was planned and prepared for you in heaven will come to pass on earth. May Matthew 6:10, "Thy kingdom come, Thy will be done in earth, as it is in heaven," be true in your life. May every promise, vision, and heavenly desire in you come to pass, in Jesus' name.

The baby was born on July 28, 2010, and we named him Jonathon, meaning, "God is gracious" or "God has given us this." We rejoiced greatly. It felt as though everything was turning around for us. Things were so good, and it was the season and the time for things to fall into place.

Nevertheless, I had a song in my spirit that took a different angle, "Blessings" by Laura Story.

One line says: "But what if your blessings come through raindrops? What if your healing comes through tears?"

The Lord told me, "You are asking for blessings, but what if these blessings come through raindrops and through your tears?"

Through this song, the Lord was preparing me for what was coming next. Two days after Jonathon's birth, the nurse informed me, "We are sorry to give you this news, but the baby has a birth defect."

With pain in my heart, I asked the Lord, "Why, Lord, why is this happening now? Whose fault is this?" I asked Him these and many other questions about Jonathon's future and how this defect would affect his life. I needed a Savior to rescue me from this dark pit, and through my mother, the Lord sent a word of knowledge and wisdom.

While I was in the hospital, crying and questioning what was going on, my mother called and said, "Cindy, I have a word from the Lord to Jonathon."

My mother had not yet heard the news about the birth defect, but she told me, "Read Psalm 139:13–16." I did, and this is what I read:

For thou hast possessed my reins: thou hast covered me in my mother's womb. I will praise thee; for I am fearfully and wonderfully made: marvelous are thy works; and that my soul knoweth right well. My substance was not hid from thee, when I was made in secret, and curiously wrought in the lowest parts of the earth. Thine eyes did see my substance, yet being imperfect; and in thy book all my members were written, which in continuance were fashioned, when as yet there was none of them.

In that moment, everything changed. The Word rescued me, and I started seeing light in this situation. I knew the Lord had allowed this to happen, and the Lord had created this baby while he was in my womb. Though people or doctors might say, "This is a birth defect," or "This is not normal," I could see my son was wonderfully and fearfully made by God Almighty. With that realization, I began rejoicing for all the great things the Lord had planned for this baby. To this day, Jonathon has already had four surgeries, and he will need more in the future. However, I continue to trust the Lord day by day, and I know that as big as this situation is, our God is bigger, mightier, and stronger.

A great lesson I learned while I was in the hospital was from Job, chapter one. I read that after all Job's losses, he "fell down" (verse 20), and that touched me deeply because I felt as if I was falling down. But the Bible didn't say he fell down and felt sorry for himself, or fell down and cried, or fell down and questioned God. The Bible says he fell down and worshiped. Similarly, in my moment of trial, I could do nothing but lift my hands to the Lord and worship. During Jonathon's surgeries, I kept singing one particular song over and over; I call it Jonathon's song. The song says:

> I'll praise you in this storm
> And I will lift my hands
> That you are who you are
> No matter where I am
> And every tear I've cried
> You hold in your hand
> You never left my side . . .
> I will praise you in this storm.

Amen.

Chapter 10

Overcomer

And they overcame him by the blood of the Lamb and by the word of their testimony.

Revelation 12:11 (KJV)

After believing and following the Lord Jesus Christ, our faith immediately will be activated to overcome this world and everything we face. "For whatsoever is born of God overcometh the world: and this is the victory that overcometh the world, even our faith. Who is he that overcometh the world, but he that believeth that Jesus is the Son of God?" (1 John 5:4–5, KJV).

God has promised that by faith we can overcome this world with all its struggles and temptations. He has given us authority to overcome the enemy: "And these signs shall follow them that believe; in my name shall they cast out devils; they shall speak with new tongues; they shall take up serpents; and if they drink any deadly thing, it shall not hurt them; they shall lay hands on the sick, and they shall recover" (Mark 16:17–18, KJV). According to this passage, the first sign that follows a believer is to cast out and defeat the enemy. After we defeat the enemy and overcome his snares, the other signs and wonders will be present in a powerful way.

My son Daniel is filled with the Holy Spirit. The Lord has anointed him in the same way the prophet Daniel was anointed. He is a praying boy, and the Lord has given him many visions and dreams.

Around 2012, when he was seven years old, he woke me up and said, "Mom, why were you wearing black and standing in the room with your back bent?"

I said I was not, and really, that night I was not wearing black.

He continued, saying, "When I came closer, I felt it was you, but really it wasn't. I was confused and afraid."

Immediately the Lord revealed to me it was a spirit that wanted to attack my life and bend me. This is the enemy's goal: to bend all Christians.

After Daniel's vision, the Lord gave me a dream, which He instructed me to share in this book. In the dream, I was with hundreds of believers in a demonic atmosphere. I saw Christians playing with lions and asked them, "Why are you playing with them? They can attack you, hurt you, and kill you."

They answered, "No, these are friendly lions. We are just playing."

After a while, the lions took authority over these individuals. They built a fence so no one could run away. They commanded the people to bow to them. All the people bowed, bent over. I too bowed and asked, "What's going to happen?"

The other Christians said to me, "The lions are going to pick their prey."

I straightened up and began to run, declaring, "I can't bend to the lions. I can't be their prey!"

I then woke up and, in my spirit, felt so sad for Christians who play with lions. They want to play and be friends with the enemy, but they don't expect to get hurt or eaten. They give all kinds of excuses for playing with the lions, saying things like, "It's okay," "They are my friends," "It's not hurting anyone," or, "It's not affecting me; I know my limits."

My Bible, however, clearly says, "Abstain from all appearance of evil" (1 Thessalonians 5:22, KJV); and "Wash you, make you clean, put away the evil of your doings from before mine eyes; cease to do evil" (Isaiah 1:16, KJV).

Furthermore, in the Old Testament, Joshua said to the people, "Sanctify yourselves: For tomorrow the Lord will do wonders among you" (Joshua 3:5, KJV). Also, Numbers 16:26 says, "Depart, I pray you, from the tents of these wicked men, and touch nothing of theirs." The most high God, the

Holy One, has called us to be separated, sanctified, Holy Ghost-filled Christians; and when we walk in holiness and separation, we will have the power to overcome the enemy.

Jesus has the power to loosen you from your infirmities, just as He did when He set free a bent woman in the temple. This woman came to church, but still she was bent. She served the Lord, but still she was bent. She prayed every day, but still she was bent by the enemy. For eighteen years, she went in and out of the house of God, but she remained bent by the enemy. Praise the Lord, though, when Jesus saw her, He told her, "Women, thou art loosed from thy infirmity," and for the first time, she saw the face of her Savior, deliverer, and healer. Hallelujah!

I label that woman today an overcomer. She kept pressing on until she got her healing. She won the battle over the enemy. If you have been through fiery trials, struggled with strongholds or addictions, or endured unjust attacks, don't be deceived. Yes, the devil is a serpent, a liar, and yes, he is a murderer from the beginning, but he knows he has only a short time: "For the devil is come down unto you having great wrath because he knoweth he hath but a short time" (Revelation 12:12, KJV). I declare, in Jesus' name, that his time in your life is over. You are free, and I label you an overcomer.

For many reasons, I believe the most important message in the Bible is the message of the overcomer in Revelation. First, it comes from a person who was not only a disciple of Jesus, but also called the beloved: "Now there was leaning on Jesus' bosom one of his disciples, whom Jesus loved" (John 13:23, KJV). He was close to Jesus' heart, so this message came from Jesus' heart to ours.

Second, the message of the overcomer is mentioned at the end of the Bible, in the book of Revelation, so that we will remember it. There are many important messages all through the Bible about faith, healing, blessing, and our walk with God; but at the end of the book, the message the

Lord wants us to remember is that He overcame and will give us the victory to overcome. Being an overcomer doesn't mean we are strong, holy, or complete; it merely means we are facing some struggles in our lives and overcoming them.

I'm going to share now about the seven churches in Revelation and the struggles they faced. Each church presents the struggles and issues that believers will face in their journeys here on earth.

1. *Leaving their first love*: "Nevertheless I have somewhat against thee, because thou hast left thy first love" (Revelation 2:4, KJV).

2. *Suffering for the faith*: "Fear none of these things which thou shalt suffer: behold, the devil shall cast some of you into prison, that ye may be tried; and ye shall have tribulation ten days: be thou faithful unto death, and I will give thee a crown of life" (Revelation 2:10, KJV).

3. *Being in places where Satan's seat is*: "I know thy works, and where thou dwellest, even where Satan's seat is: and thou holdest fast my name, and hast not denied my faith" (Revelation 2:13, KJV).

4. *Being tempted with fornication*: "Notwithstanding I have a few things against thee, because thou sufferest that woman Jezebel, which calleth herself a prophetess, to teach and to seduce my servants to commit fornication, and to eat things sacrificed unto idols" (Revelation 2:20, KJV).

5. *Works not perfect before God*: "Be watchful, and strengthen the things which remain, that are ready to die: for I have not found thy works perfect before God" (Revelation 3:2, KJV).

6. *Facing temptation*: "Because thou hast kept the word of my patience, I also will keep thee from the hour of temptation, which

shall come upon all the world" (Revelation 3:10, KJV).

7. *Being neither cold nor hot and not feeling a need for God*: "I know thy works, that thou art neither cold nor hot: I would thou wert cold or hot" (Revelation 3:15, KJV).

When we overcome, our heavenly Father promises these blessings to our lives:

- "To him that overcometh will I give to eat of the tree of life" (Revelation 2:7, KJV).
- "He that overcometh shall not be hurt of the second death" (Revelation 2:11, KJV).
- "To him that overcometh will I give to eat of the hidden manna" (Revelation 2:17, KJV).
- "And he that overcometh to him will I give power over the nations" (Revelation 2:26, KJV).
- "He that overcometh shall be clothed in white" (Revelation 3:5).

- "Him that overcometh will I make a pillar in the temple of my God" (Revelation 3:12, KJV).
- "To him that overcometh will I grant to sit with me in my throne even as I also overcame" (Revelation 3:21, KJV).

All the tribulation, temptation, pain, sorrow, failure, and sickness we face are chances for us to overcome—to overcome by the blood of the Lamb and the word of our testimony. I want you to imagine, right now with me, you and me wearing white: "He that overcometh shall be clothed in white" (Revelation 3:5, KJV). I want you to imagine us walking with Jesus and hearing Him say to each of us, "You are worthy," for "they shall walk with me in white: for they are worthy" (Revelation 3:4, KJV). He will call us worthy because we overcame.

So, when you see me one day in heaven walking in these white clothes, you will know that I am an overcomer. Yes, I suffered. Yes, I was tempted. Yes, I was weak. Yes, I was lonely. Yes, I had my fears, burdens, and worries. Yes, I was sick. Yes, I was in jail. Yes, I was rejected. Yes, I was depressed. But I am an overcomer, and so are you. You are called to be an overcomer.

CPSIA information can be obtained
at www.ICGtesting.com
Printed in the USA
FSHW02n0641130718